IMAGES OF T
NATIONAL ARChivɛs

PRIME MINISTERS
OF THE
20TH CENTURY

Dedicated to the memory of John Nugent Dunton

IMAGES OF THE NATIONAL ARCHIVES

PRIME MINISTERS
OF THE
20TH CENTURY

MARK DUNTON

PEN & SWORD HISTORY

AN IMPRINT OF PEN & SWORD BOOKS LTD.
YORKSHIRE – PHILADELPHIA

First published in Great Britain in 2021 by
Pen and Sword History
An imprint of
Pen & Sword Books Ltd
Yorkshire - Philadelphia

ISBN 978 1 52672 949 1

Typeset in Minion Pro 11/14.5 by
SJmagic DESIGN SERVICES, India.

Printed and bound in the Uk by CPI Group (UK) Ltd. Croydon, CR0 4YY.

Pen & Sword Books Ltd incorporates the Imprints of Pen & Sword Books Archaeology, Atlas, Aviation, Battleground, Discovery, Family History, History, Maritime, Military, Naval, Politics, Railways, Select, Transport, True Crime, Fiction, Frontline Books, Leo Cooper, Praetorian Press, Seaforth Publishing, Wharncliffe and White Owl.

For a complete list of Pen & Sword titles please contact

PEN & SWORD BOOKS LIMITED
47 Church Street, Barnsley, South Yorkshire, S70 2AS, England
E-mail: enquiries@pen-and-sword.co.uk
Website: www.pen-and-sword.co.uk

or

PEN AND SWORD BOOKS
1950 Lawrence Rd, Havertown, PA 19083, USA
E-mail: Uspen-and-sword@casematepublishers.com
Website: www.penandswordbooks.com

CONTENTS

ACKNOWLEDGEMENTS

I would like to thank Mark Pearsall and Dr Stephen Twigge for their helpful advice during the drafting process. I would also like to thank Ela Kaczmarska, Publishing Executive at The National Archives, and Aileen Pringle, Carol Trow and Janet Brookes of Pen & Sword, for all they have done to make this book possible.

Mark Dunton, April 2020

INTRODUCTION

The Prime Minister is at the apex of power in government. He or she has ultimate responsibility for governmental decisions, chairs the Cabinet, drives the political agenda, and appoints and dismisses ministers. The Prime Minister also advises the Sovereign when Parliament should be dissolved and a general election held.

By common consensus, the first of the line was Sir Robert Walpole, who served from 1721 to 1742, but the title of Prime Minister was not acknowledged formally until 1878. The powers and duties of the role are not defined by any statute; the office of Prime Minister has evolved over time, accruing new functions, customs and conventions. Herbert Asquith declared that 'the office … is what its holder chooses and is able to make of it'.

The wisdom of Asquith's dictum becomes apparent as you peruse the history of the individual Prime Ministers. The variety of personalities who have held this office in the twentieth century is striking. Very neatly there are twenty (some had more than one premiership). Images of documents from The National Archives give insights into their characters, how they projected themselves, and the formidable challenges they faced. Some were unlucky; others made their own luck.

In many ways, for all the prestige associated with the role, it is an unenviable job, subject to huge pressures, and this selection of documents show our Prime Ministers grappling with all manner of problems. All is not angst and frustration, however; there are instances where wit is deployed to great effect.

As well as the decline of the British Empire, the twentieth century saw two world wars and the development of the welfare state. Government acquired a greater role in national life, and this was reflected in the importance of the Prime Ministerial role. Party considerations also became increasingly important, and the way that the public perceived a government became bound up with the performance of its Prime Minister. The names of the Prime Ministers of the twentieth century are the chapter headings of Britain's modern history.

ROBERT GASCOYNE-CECIL, 3RD MARQUESS OF SALISBURY

Born: 3 February 1830
Died: 22 August 1903
Dates in Office: 23 June 1885 – 28 January 1886
                 25 July 1886 – 11 August 1892
                 25 June 1895 – 11 July 1902
Party: Conservative

The Marquis of Salisbury, 1887. *COPY 1/77*

You might be tempted to assume that Lord Salisbury, a figure from a privileged background who rose to the pinnacle of political power, had a charmed and gilded life. But look at this image of Lord Salisbury around the age of 57, and what do you see? There is a melancholy look in his eyes: he gives an impression of vulnerability and great seriousness. What lay behind this aura of sadness?

As a boy, Robert Cecil loved books and subjects such as botany, theology and the sciences. He had a lonely childhood with few friends and occupied himself with reading. He disliked sports and had no interest in traditional country pursuits such as shooting. At the age of eleven, Cecil went to Eton College. His sensitive, bookish and intellectual nature set him apart from other boys, and he was subjected to ferocious bullying, to such an extent that, with his mental and physical health close to collapse, his father withdrew him from the school at the age of fifteen.

Lord Salisbury's troubled passage to adulthood marked him for life. Through his experiences, Cecil developed a very pessimistic view of human nature and the cruelty of the mob. This outlook helps to explain his opposition to the Second Reform Bill (the Reform Act of 1867), which enfranchised the majority of men who lived in urban areas in England and Wales.

Dislike of mob mentality also helps to explain his disdain for jingoism. Although the British Empire expanded massively during his premierships, he has been referred to as a reluctant imperialist. While his final premiership saw the intensely bitter and bloody Boer War in South Africa, he managed to bring this to a generally acceptable conclusion on 31 May 1902.

The Relief of Mafeking in South Africa is announced in this *Daily Telegraph* billboard in Trafalgar Square, London on 19 May 1900 (see page 10). The British garrison at Mafeking, numbering about 2,000 and led by Colonel Robert Baden-Powell, had been under siege for seven months by a 5,000-strong Boer force. The news that the siege was broken gave a great morale boost to the British after earlier military disasters.

Newspaper vendor in Trafalgar Square, London, 19 May 1900. *COPY 1/447*

'The use of Conservatism is to delay changes till they become harmless.'

Robert Gascoyne-Cecil,
3rd Marquess of Salisbury

ARTHUR JAMES BALFOUR

Born: 25 July 1848
Died: 19 March 1930
Dates in Office: 12 July 1902 – 4 December 1905
Party: Conservative

Arthur Balfour, 1903. *COPY 1/467*

Arthur Balfour was highly intelligent; he possessed a sceptical, enquiring mind, and a deep interest in philosophy. However, he was also indecisive, and lacking in leadership qualities, as evidenced by his approach to the key issue of his premiership, free trade.

Joseph Chamberlain, Colonial Secretary from 1895 to 1903 (who served in this role under Salisbury and then Balfour) campaigned vigorously on 'tariff reform'. He believed that the best way of consolidating the Empire was to give preferential trading terms to its members, while imposing high tariffs on other suppliers, thus ending free trade. However, several members of Balfour's Cabinet were convinced of the value of free trade.

Balfour had no strong views on the matter. He was sympathetic to the notion of placing duties on imports, with preferential arrangements to protect the British colonies. However, he was acutely aware of the drawbacks, not least the likelihood that food prices would rise. He developed subtle 'half-way house' formulations, involving retaliatory tariffs, to be used if faced with protectionism from other countries. He tried to postpone debate on this controversial issue and failed to give a lead on it. His equivocal approach pleased no one, and in September 1903, five Cabinet members resigned over the issue, including Joseph Chamberlain. Balfour was a superb analyst; but he lacked leadership qualities.

Extract from handwritten letter from A J Balfour to Edward VII concerning Tariff Reform, 15 September 1903. *CAB 41/28*

'It is difficult because a bargain is always difficult: it is especially difficult because it is hard to see how any bargain could be contrived which the Colonies would accept, and which would not involve some taxation on food in this country.'

Despite his personal flaws, Balfour's record as Prime Minister was not devoid of achievements. It can be argued that his chief accomplishment was the Education Act of 1902. This Act abolished the school boards and transferred control of elementary education to newly established Local Education Authorities (LEAs), with schools funded out of local taxation. The measure did cause controversy – it was opposed by non-conformists who saw it an instrument for aiding Anglican schools; however, it is seen by historians as a landmark. In the words of Balfour biographer E.H.H. Green, 'The 1902 Act did see the introduction of the first truly national educational system in Britain.'

He is most famous for the Balfour Declaration of November 1917, which expressed the British Government's support for 'the establishment in Palestine of a national home for the Jewish people' on the understanding that nothing shall be done which may prejudice the civil and religious rights of existing non-Jewish communities in Palestine'. The repercussions of this Declaration reverberate to the present day.

'Nothing matters very much, and very few things matter at all.'

Arthur James Balfour

SIR HENRY CAMPBELL-BANNERMAN

Born: 7 September 1836
Died: 22 April 1908
Dates in Office: 5 December 1905 – 5 April 1908
Party: Liberal

Sir Henry Campbell-Bannerman, 1907. *COPY 1/508/102*

Sir Henry Campbell-Bannerman is one of the least well-remembered Prime Ministers of the twentieth century, even though his brief premiership featured several notable achievements, including the Trade Disputes Act, 1906, which provided trade unions with immunity from liability for damages arising from strike actions, and the Probation of Offenders Act 1907, which laid down the foundations of the probation service. He brought about a generous reconciliation with the Boers in South Africa. He was also the only Prime Minister to die at No. 10: ill health forced him to resign, but he remained in No. 10 until he died almost three weeks later.

Why isn't 'CB', as he styled himself, better known? The chief reason is his lack of flamboyance. He lacked the gift of fine oratory, and, for much of his career, he was a poor performer in the Commons. He was seen as dull and plodding, yet also as an efficient administrator with a great deal of common sense.

This lack of effusiveness showed itself in his letters to Edward VII. Before the advent of Cabinet Minutes, the Prime Minister was expected to write a private letter to the Sovereign after each Cabinet meeting, to give an account of proceedings. Disraeli's letters to Queen Victoria were effusive and lengthy; many of Campbell-Bannerman's letters to Edward VII were concise to the point of sounding terse. Occasionally, the King wrote sarcastic responses on these letters – there were times when he was plainly unhappy at the minimal information. This can be seen in CB's letter to Edward VII dated 9 April 1906:

'Sir Henry Campbell-Bannerman, with his humble duty, begs to report to your Majesty that the Cabinet met today for a short time in order to adjust two difficulties of detail which had been found in the draft Education Act relating to tests for teachers, and the hours and conditions of religious teaching.'

The King commented at the top of the letter with heavy sarcasm: 'What valuable information.'

> 'When is a war not a war? When it is carried on by methods of barbarism in South Africa.'
>
> Sir Henry Campbell-Bannerman

What valuable information
k.B.

10, Downing Street,
Whitehall. S.W.

Sir Henry Campbell Bannerman, with his humble duty, begs to report to Your Majesty that the Cabinet met today for a short time in order to adjust two difficulties of detail which had been found in the draft Education Act, relating to tests for teachers, and the hours and conditions of religious teaching.

9 April. 06   Rec: April 17/06

Campbell-Bannerman's letter to Edward VII, 9 April 1906. *CAB 41/30*

HERBERT ASQUITH

Born: 12 September 1852
Died: 15 February 1928
Dates in Office: 7 April 1908 – 5 December 1916
Party: Liberal

Herbert Henry Asquith, 1910. *COPY 1/552*

On 24 July 1911, Prime Minister Herbert Asquith rose to address the House of Commons, and was immediately assailed with Opposition cries of 'Traitor'. He rose to speak several times, unable to even begin his speech, and when he managed to make a start, he was rudely and frequently interrupted, so much so that, after half an hour, he sat down, unheard – an extraordinary occasion for a Prime Minister. How had this come to pass?

Asquith was appointed Chancellor of the Exchequer in the Liberal Government which came to power in 1906. Here he was at the top of his game – a master of the detail – and introduced budgetary reforms, a graduated income tax, and the first provisions which brought about old age pensions. He was also a brilliant performer in the Commons, making every point count. When Campbell-Bannerman resigned (shortly before he died at No. 10), Asquith was the natural successor as Prime Minister.

Chancellor David Lloyd George's 'People's Budget' of 1909 was designed to tax the wealthy in order to pay for increased defence and welfare reforms. When the Lords rejected this budget, Asquith backed his Chancellor to the hilt and the issue became a huge showdown between the Commons and the Lords.

The Lords eventually passed the 'People's Budget', but Asquith raised the stakes by introducing the Parliament Bill, restricting the powers of the House of Lords. He managed to secure a promise from the new king, George V, to create hundreds of new Liberal peers if the Parliament Bill was not passed by the Lords; this remained a secret for a while. In July 1911, his announcement of the agreement with the king led to the furore in the Commons described earlier, with noisy and strident opposition from those who wanted the aristocratic power of the Lords to remain undiluted. But Asquith succeeded – eventually the Parliament Act was passed without the creation of new peers.

Although Asquith certainly had credentials as a social reformer, at the time of the Suffragettes campaign he was opposed to extending the vote to women, though he changed his position in voting for the Representation of the People Act in 1918.

During the First World War, Asquith was not an effective war leader: he was strangely passive and became associated with the catchphrase 'wait and see'. He lacked a sense of urgency, and a proper grip on strategy. The death of his son Raymond on the Somme in September 1916 had a shattering effect on him and at times he had difficulties controlling his drinking, leading to some embarrassing scenes in the Commons. He also conducted flirtatious relationships with several young women; for example, he became infatuated with the aristocrat and socialite Venetia Stanley.

The war outlook continued to be gloomy and after various intrigues involving David Lloyd George, Asquith was forced to resign in December 1916.

Suffragettes Jessie Kenney and Miss Vera Wentworth confront Prime Minister Asquith about votes for women, as depicted by *The Illustrated London News* of 28 November 1908. *ZPER 34/133*

'We are within measurable, or imaginable, distance of a real Armageddon. Happily there seems to be no reason why we should be anything more than spectators.'

(Written by Herbert Asquith as Europe was on the brink of war, 24 July 1914).

DAVID LLOYD GEORGE

Born: 17 January 1863
Died: 26 March 1945
Dates in Office: 6 December 1916 – 19 October 1922
Party: Liberal

David Lloyd George, 1906. *COPY 1/493*

David Lloyd George in his prime stares directly at you. Looking at this photograph from 1906 you can appreciate the contemporary accounts of his magnetism, and sense his force of personality and self-belief. This image captures him so vividly that you can imagine he is about to speak directly to you. He projects a strong self-confidence: but it was over-confidence that ultimately contributed to his political downfall.

Lloyd George had many achievements to his name. As a social reformer, and as Chancellor of the Exchequer, he introduced old age pensions in 1908. He overcame considerable resistance to create the National Insurance in 1911, which provided for sick pay and unemployment insurance.

Following a scandal about a shortage of shells, Lloyd George was appointed Minister of Munitions in May 1915. He was incredibly successful in leading his new Ministry, massively increasing the output of shells and other armaments.

When Lloyd George became Prime Minister in December 1916, (replacing Asquith as head of the wartime coalition government), he hit the ground running. He formed a small war cabinet of five members and immediately introduced a far more business-like approach to government, appointing the first Cabinet Secretary, Sir Maurice Hankey, to take formal minutes of meetings for the first time. The Cabinet Office duly emerged, and Lloyd George also appointed special advisors who worked in huts in the garden of No. 10 (the 'Garden Suburb').

Lloyd George was a vigorous war leader, making determined efforts to boost industrial efficiency and farm production. He backed the introduction of a rationing system and he set up new ministries headed by decisive and talented appointees. There were significant limits to Lloyd George's ability to control military strategy – operations remained largely the preserve of the generals, and he had a poor relationship with the British Commander-in-Chief, Sir Douglas Haig. However, when the war ended in November 1918, Lloyd George was widely praised as 'the man who won the war'. Certainly his success in mobilising Britain's human and material resources, and his determination to see the war through to the end, were vital factors contributing to victory.

After the war, Lloyd George remained Prime Minister, and was obviously an important player at the Versailles conference, though his attempts to moderate punitive measures being imposed on Germany were unsuccessful. With regard to the long running issue of Irish Home Rule (self-government for Ireland), Lloyd George did achieve the compromise solution of partition, implemented in 1921, but in general the post-war period was a difficult time for him.

His style of governing became more and more presidential; he became detached from the Liberal Party, having alienated many former colleagues, and increasingly, he irritated his Conservative colleagues who dominated the government. Lloyd George's standing

WC 500 B
11 Nov/18

305

(1) The Prime Minister announced that he had received a message from France stating that the armistice had been signed at
5 a.m. that morning, November 11th., 1918, and that hostilities
were to cease six hours later, viz., 11 a.m. He wished to consult his colleagues as to whether the public announcement of the
signing of the armistice should be made at once and the form it
should take.

After a brief discussion the War Cabinet decided —

(a) That the announcement should be made at once
    through the Press Bureau, to the effect that
    the armistice was signed at 5 a.m. and hostil-
    ities were to cease at 11 a.m. today:

(b) That the Commander-in-Chief of the Home Forces
    should at once inform all Home Commands, and
    should take the necessary steps to celebrate
    the news by the firing of maroons, playing of
    bands, blowing of bugles, and ringing of
    Church bells throughout the Kingdom:

(c) Similarly the First Lord should arrange for
    vessels of the Fleet to dress ship:

(d) That the order prohibiting the striking of
    Church and other public clocks should be at
    once rescinded, the Home Secretary to take
    the necessary action:

(e) That the terms of the armistice should not be
    made public until they had been communicated
    by the Prime Minister to the House of Commons
    simultaneously with a similar pronouncement by
    M. Clemenceau in the Chamber of Deputies:

(f) The Press Bureau to be informed accordingly.

Minutes of Cabinet Meeting, 11 November 1918. *CAB 23/14, WC 500b*

was damaged by a scandal over his granting of honours in return for donations to party funds. These problems arising from a rather reckless approach are indicative of the over-inflated sense of self-confidence mentioned earlier. In October 1922, the Conservatives withdrew their support for the coalition, and Lloyd George resigned. The general election of 1922 produced a Conservative majority and the Liberal Party as a political force went into significant decline.

> 'The finest eloquence is that which gets things done.'
>
> David Lloyd George

ANDREW BONAR LAW

Born: 16 September 1858
Died: 30 October 1923
Dates in Office: 23 October 1922 – 20 May 1923
Party: Conservative

Andrew Bonar Law, 1912. *COPY1/564/179*

Bonar Law is often portrayed as dour, but that isn't the impression conveyed by this photograph, dated 1912, in which his eyes are smiling, and he looks engaged and alert. He *did* possess a sociable side to his nature – he spent a great deal of time in the smoking rooms with his MPs (his love of cigars contributed to his untimely death). It should also be remembered that he got on very well with David Lloyd George, so it is safe to assume he had qualities of wit and charm, particularly when he relaxed, even if he was not a 'showy' personality.

Andrew Taylor has written: 'Bonar Law's natural melancholia was exacerbated by personal tragedy'. He was devastated by the sudden death of his wife, Annie, in 1909, and the loss of two sons in the First World War. Following these bereavements, he increasingly sought comfort in his work.

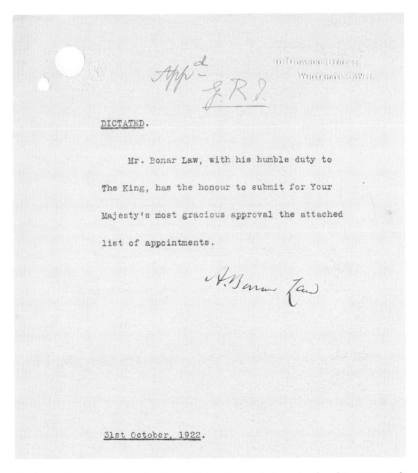

Andrew Bonar Law submits a list of appointments for his Majesty's approval, as he forms his Conservative government in October 1922.
PREM 5/196

<u>Air Ministry, Secretary of State</u>.

Sir Samuel Hoare, Bart., C.M.G.

<u>Minister of Labour</u>.

Sir Montague Barlow, K.B.E.

<u>Minister of Pensions</u>.

G. C. Tryon Esq.

<u>First Commissioner of Works</u>.

Sir John Baird, Bart., C.M.G., D.S.O.

<u>Solicitor General</u>.

T. W. H. Inskip Esq., C.B.E., K.C.

<u>Postmaster General</u>.

Neville Chamberlain Esq.

<u>Under Secretary of State for Home Affairs</u>.

The Hon. G. F. Stanley, C.M.G.

<u>Under Secretary of State for Foreign Affairs</u>.

Ronald McNeill Esq.

<u>Under Secretary of State for the Colonies</u>.

The Hon. W. Ormsby-Gore.

<u>Under Secretary of State for War</u>.

The Hon. Walter Guinness, D.S.O.

<u>Financial Secretary to the War Office</u>.

The Hon. F. S. Jackson.

<u>Under Secretary, Air Ministry</u>.

The Duke of Sutherland.

<u>Under Secretary of State for India</u>.

Earl Winterton.

Extract from Andrew Bonar Law's list of appointments. *PREM 5/196*

There are certain facts about Bonar Law which distinguish him. His premiership lasted a mere 209 days, and this serves to explain – at least in part – the unfortunate epithet (coined by Asquith) 'the unknown Prime Minister'. He was also the only twentieth century Prime Minister to be born abroad, in New Brunswick, Canada.

On the outbreak of the First World War, Law had accepted the need for national unity, and in May 1915 he joined the Liberals in coalition, becoming Colonial Secretary. A close working relationship and friendship with David Lloyd George developed. Law effectively helped Lloyd George become Prime Minister in December 1916, and in this new administration, Law became Chancellor of the Exchequer, and Leader of the House of Commons. It was a very effective political alliance.

Following Lloyd George's resignation and the collapse of the coalition in October 1922, Law was invited to form a Conservative government. He immediately called a general election, to be held on 15 November. Law proposed a 'tranquillity manifesto' to enable Britain to recover from the war, and the Conservatives won a comfortable majority.

During his short premiership, Law's approach to government was very narrow. He desired a minimal role for the state, and was unenthusiastic about social reform. It was a case of steady as she goes, with policies that could be described as 'laissez faire'. His strategy was limited and unimaginative.

Law's premiership came to an end in May 1923 when he resigned due to ill health. He died of throat cancer on 30 October 1923.

> 'I am afraid I shall have to show myself very vicious, Mr Asquith, this session. I hope you will understand.' (Andrew Bonar Law speaking at the 1912 State Opening of Parliament, as reported by Herbert Asquith).

STANLEY BALDWIN

Born: 3 August 1867
Died: 14 December 1947
Dates in Office: 23 May 1923 – 16 January 1924
                   4 November 1924 – 5 June 1929
                   7 June 1935 – 28 May 1937
Party: Conservative

On the previous day, December 3rd, he was to have seen the King at 6 p.m., but he received a message from the King's Valet asking him to come to Buckingham Palace secretly at 9 p.m. He had driven there and had been taken in by a back entrance; but all the same he had been photographed. Then he had been introduced through a window. Sir Godfrey Thomas had awaited him, looking twenty years older. On this occasion the King came back to his idea of a broadcast which he wanted to make this very evening (December 4th). His Majesty had read to the Prime Minister a draft and had said he thought it right, before he abdicated, that on behalf of Mrs Simpson and himself he should say what they wanted to do. He had been frantically keen to do this and had said that he felt sure the Prime Minister knew at heart that he was right in this. The Prime Minister had replied that it was a matter of the Constitution and that he would have to consult the Cabinet. Making clear that he was speaking informally, he had reminded the King of what he had told him as to the attitude of his Cabinet colleagues, the Party Leaders in Parliament and the Prime Ministers of the Dominions: adding that now the King proposed to go over the heads of his

Baldwin's account of his visit to the King given to the Cabinet on 4 December 1936. *CAB 23/86, CC 70 (36)*

Prime Minister Stanley Baldwin informed his Cabinet about a secret visit to King Edward VIII which had taken place on 3 December 1936. The news that the King wished to marry the twice divorced American, Wallis Simpson, had just broken in the British press. In this extraordinary account, Baldwin states that he had to enter Buckingham Palace via a back entrance and a window, such was the level of secrecy involved.

Edward VIII, 1936. *TS 22/1/1*

Edward wanted to deliver a radio broadcast to the British people about his intention to marry Mrs Simpson (and remain king) – in effect this would be an appeal to the public over the heads of the government – but Baldwin felt duty bound to point out the constitutional dangers of this, and the Cabinet refused to allow the King to carry out this plan.

To the British establishment, the prospect of a twice divorced American woman becoming Queen was unacceptable. Baldwin made every effort to allow Edward to re-consider his wish to marry Wallis Simpson, but when it became clear that Edward's mind was made up, the Prime Minister took a firm line and refused to support plans which would have allowed him to marry and remain king. This complex matter necessitated several difficult conversations with the king, and Baldwin deployed the full range of his personal qualities to help resolve the matter: a mixture of tact, sensitivity, sympathy and frankness. He also managed to consult with senior ministers, Parliament, the Dominions and the Archbishop of Canterbury *and* hold the line with the press as long as possible. Edward made up his mind to abdicate and could not be shifted from that position; he duly signed the Instrument of Abdication on 10 December 1936.

Stanley Baldwin. *Library of Congress*

Baldwin's careful handling of the abdication crisis in 1936 brought him credit, and boosted his popularity with the public. His handling of an earlier crisis, the General Strike in 1926, was also well received and although he took a firm line, his pronouncements were moderate in tone and he emerged as a healer of divisions. Baldwin's hero was Disraeli and his 'one nation conservatism', making an appeal which cut across class barriers, placing emphasis on national unity. He was a very effective communicator and perfected the cosy and reassuring 'fireside chat' in his radio broadcasts.

However, his reputation suffered severe damage from 1940 onwards. That year – when the 'phoney war' became very real – was obviously a very difficult time for Britain. A popular polemical book entitled *The Guilty Men* placed much of the blame for the unpreparedness of British military forces upon Baldwin, as well as other prominent members of the National Government. The search for a scapegoat became particular acute after the death of Chamberlain in October 1940 and Baldwin found himself subjected to heavy criticism about his perceived slowness to respond to the challenge from Hitler and the Nazis in the 1930s.

> 'I want to see a better feeling between all classes of our people … I want to be a healer.'
>
> Stanley Baldwin

RAMSAY MACDONALD

Born:	12 October 1866
Died:	9 November 1937
Dates in Office:	22 January 1924 – 4 November 1924
	5 June 1929 – 7 June 1935
Party:	Labour

Ramsay MacDonald and Lady Londonderry. *PRO 30/69/1674*

Ramsay MacDonald and Lady Londonderry take a break during a walk in the countryside in this photograph which is thought to date from the early 1930s. When they first met at a dinner at Buckingham Palace, no one could have predicted that they would have become such close friends. Edith, Lady Londonderry was a rich conservative at the apex of high society. Ramsay was Britain's first-ever Labour Prime Minister, who had risen from humble origins, and was of modest means. Her husband, Charles, was a coalmine owner; MacDonald believed the coal mines should be taken into public ownership. What did they have in common? For one thing, they were both Scottish, and shared a love of Highland culture.

MacDonald was a widower. When his wife Margaret died from blood poisoning in 1911, he was devastated, and thereafter, he craved emotional support and developed intense friendships with several women, including Lady Margaret Sackville, the writer

Ramsay MacDonald, 1924. *PRO 30/69/1668*

and society beauty. Several years on from their first meeting in 1924, Ramsay came to find Edith a particularly charming and joyful presence and he later became entranced with the world of glittering dinner parties at Londonderry House, at which Edith was the hostess par excellence.

MacDonald became the first ever Labour Prime Minister in January 1924, as head of a minority government. He steered clear of radical socialist measures; at a time when there were widespread fears about communism, he was anxious to appear moderate. His main priority was to demonstrate that Labour could govern in a competent fashion. MacDonald and his ministers wore court dress for their meetings with the King; this brought some mockery which MacDonald dismissed.

He took the role of Foreign Secretary as well as Prime Minister and engaged in foreign affairs with a measure of success. MacDonald's first experience of power lasted less than ten months, before he was replaced by Baldwin.

In June 1929, MacDonald returned to power, again as Prime Minister of a minority government. To many urban working class voters at this time, MacDonald was the personification of all their hopes for a better life, but his government's cautious attempts to reduce unemployment were overtaken by events. The Wall Street Crash of October 1929 prompted a world-wide slump and unemployment soared. MacDonald's government had no real answer to the problem and were sceptical about the programmes of public works advocated by John Maynard Keynes, David Lloyd George and others.

In the summer of 1931, the financial crisis took an even worse turn and significant expenditure cuts were proposed, including cuts in unemployment benefit. This issue caused unbridgeable divisions in the Cabinet and MacDonald offered his resignation to the king. However, George V put pressure on him to continue, as Prime Minister of an all-party coalition National Government, and MacDonald became convinced that it was his duty to do so and so he formed a new government on 24 August, which included only three other former Labour Cabinet ministers.

Macdonald was denounced as a traitor by many former Labour Party colleagues and supporters. He became isolated and the need for support was stronger than ever. His romantic obsession with Edith became very intense – this is evidenced by their correspondence – and they became the subject of gossip.

However, it is highly doubtful that the pair were lovers. As Anne De Courcy has written in *Society's Queen: The Life of Edith, Marchioness of Londonderry*, 'everything known about either of them points to the conclusion that physical love was not part of the bond that linked them'. Edith was devoted to her husband, Charles, who served as Secretary of State for Air under MacDonald, and the Prime Minister's moral code would not have allowed

367

THE FINANCIAL POSITION.

....

Resignation of the Government.

(Previous Reference: Cabinet 46 (31) Conclusion 2 (IV).).

1.   The Prime Minister informed the Cabinet that, as a result of the failure to reach agreement on the previous day, the financial position had greatly deteriorated, and the situation was now one of the gravest possible character.

As had then been arranged, His Majesty had received Mr. Baldwin, Sir Herbert Samuel and himself in audience that morning, and it was quite clear that no useful purpose would be served by consideration of any question other than that of saving the country from financial collapse. The proposal was that His Majesty would invite certain individuals, as individuals, to take upon their shoulders the burden of carrying on the Government, and Mr. Baldwin and Sir Herbert Samuel had stated that they were prepared to act accordingly.

The Prime Minister then stated that he proposed to tender to His Majesty the resignation of the Government. He had not failed to present the case against his participation in the proposed Administration, but in view of the gravity of the situation he had felt that there was no other course open to him than to assist in the formation of a National Government on a comprehensive basis for the purpose of meeting the present emergency.

The new Cabinet would be/very small one of about 12 Ministers, and the Administration would not exist for a period longer than was necessary to dispose of the emergency, and when that purpose

1.

Cabinet Minutes, 24 August 1931. *CAB 23/67, CC 47 (31)*

him to make any serious advance towards Edith, with all the danger of scandal that such a move could bring.

As MacDonald's health deteriorated during his last years in office, his outlook became increasingly morose and this put some strain on the friendship; they saw less of each other, though, fundamentally, they remained friends right up to Macdonald's death on 9 November 1937.

'Socialism marks the growth of society, not the uprising of a class.'

Ramsay MacDonald

NEVILLE CHAMBERLAIN

Born: 18 March 1869
Died: 9 November 1940
Dates in Office: 28 May 1937 – 10 May 1940
Party: Conservative

Neville Chamberlain in France, 1940. *CN 11/6 (53)*

By mid-September 1938, international tension was reaching new heights. Hitler signalled that Germany was poised to invade Czechoslovakia, on the pretext of defending the Sudeten Germans who were mostly concentrated in the Czech border regions. War seemed to be looming. Neville Chamberlain undertook, in his own words, an 'unconventional and daring' mission. On 15 September, he took his first ever flight to Germany and met Hitler for the first time at his private mountain retreat in Berchtesgaden near Munich. It was the first of several high-stakes summits which was to culminate in the Munich Agreement of 30 September. On his return from the first encounter with Hitler, Chamberlain reported back to the Cabinet.

In these short extracts from his account of the meeting given to Cabinet, one can see the seeds of Chamberlain's later fall from grace. A key sentence is 'The Prime Minister had formed the opinion that Herr Hitler's objectives were strictly limited'. With hindsight, this was a catastrophic failure of judgement, a wilful refusal to take heed of the mounting evidence to the contrary. In his dealings with Hitler, Chamberlain failed to understand that the Fuehrer was playing by another set of rules entirely, far removed from international diplomatic norms.

Another significant comment reads, 'information from other sources had been to the effect that the Fuehrer had been most favourably impressed' [by the Prime Minister]. Chamberlain had great self-belief but this was a double-edged sword, as it also amounted to over-confidence in his own judgement, bordering on vanity, and Hitler played on this.

The Munich Agreement, which permitted Germany's annexation of the Sudetenland, was combined with international safeguards regarding the remainder of Czechoslovakia. The Czechs were not consulted in any meaningful way and reluctantly gave their agreement.

On his return from Munich, Chamberlain was greeted by the majority of the public as a hero. He famously brandished the piece of paper which declared that Britain and Germany were resolved never to go to war again. There was a collective national sigh of relief that war had been averted. However, in less than six months, the Munich Agreement had unravelled – German troops marched in to the remainder of Czechoslovakia on 15 March 1939. The endgame was in sight and on 1 September, Germany invaded Poland and Britain declared war on Germany two days later. Chamberlain was devastated by the outbreak of war.

Neville Chamberlain will always be linked with two words: appeasement and Munich. The notorious Munich Agreement was seen by many as an ignoble and shameful act, which paved the way for the dismemberment of Czechoslovakia and failed to deliver Chamberlain's hopes for peace. It was the high water mark of appeasement, the diplomatic policy of making concessions to an aggressive powers in order to avoid conflict.

72

The Prime Minister said that he had no idea that this conversation would last anything approaching so long a time. What he had in mind was to open by suggesting to Herr Hitler that this was an opportunity for bringing about a new understanding between England and Germany. He had started on this line. He had said that this idea had been in his mind ever since he had been Prime Minister. Up till now various events had occurred which had rendered it impossible to make any progress, but he hoped that the opportunity had now come. The events of the last few weeks, however, had been so serious that, unless some remedy could be found, it seemed likely that his hopes of an understanding would continue to be disappointed. It was this, and not merely the troubles in Czechoslovakia, that had made him want to visit Herr Hitler. Herr Hitler had replied that the other matters to which the Prime Minister referred were of great importance, but unfortunately there was something else of the utmost urgency and could not wait, namely the Sudeten-German question. The Prime Minister had then agreed to discuss this matter.

The Prime Minister said he would like to give the impression which he had formed of Herr Hitler as the conversation proceeded. He saw no signs of insanity but many of excitement. Occasionally Herr Hitler would lose the thread of what he was saying and would go off into a tirade. It was impossible not to be impressed with the power of the man. He was extremely determined; he had thought out what he wanted and he meant to get it and he would not brook opposition beyond a certain point. Further, and this was a point of considerable importance, the Prime Minister had formed the opinion that Herr Hitler's objectives were strictly limited.

-9-

Chamberlain reports to Cabinet, 17 September 1938. *CAB 23/95, CC 39 (38)*

80

The Prime Minister thought that Herr Hitler would hold the position until the conversations had been resumed, but it was important to lose no time.

The Prime Minister emphasised that there had been no opportunity for him to put smaller points, or to try and impose conditions, or to get Herr Hitler to accept alternative solutions which seemed reasonable over here but which would not have been accepted in the atmosphere prevailing at Berchtesgarten. The only practical course had been for him to return home and consult his colleagues.

The Prime Minister concluded by saying that when he left Herr Hitler he had been uncertain what impression he had made upon him. He mentioned, however, that Herr Hitler's manner was definitely different when they left his study; he had stopped halfway down the stairs and lamented the fact that the bad weather made it impossible for him to take the Prime Minister to see the view from the top of the mountain. Herr Hitler had said that he hoped this might be possible on some other occasion. Information from other sources had been to the effect that the Fuehrer had been most favourably impressed. This was of the utmost importance, since the future conduct of these negotiations depended mainly upon personal contacts.

The Prime Minister thought that it was not possible to deal with a man such as Herr Hitler by attaching conditions. He thought, however, that if the principle of self-determination was accepted and negotiations were entered into as to the method of applying that principle, Herr Hitler would not prove too difficult about such questions as the area of the plebiscite, and the conditions under which it was to be carried out.

At the end of the conversation Herr Hitler had said that when the Czechoslovakian question was settled he would like to take up the question of Anglo-German relations and especially the question of colonies; Germany would not abandon her demand for colonies, but it was not a war matter.

-17-

Cabinet Minutes, 17 September 1938. *CAB 23/95, CC 39 (38)*

NEVILLE CHAMBERLAIN

Neville Chamberlain (Artist: Wooping). *INF 3/46*

For many decades, Chamberlain has been the subject of much ire, and it is difficult to view him dispassionately. However, we must take into account the world in which Chamberlain existed. Up to 1938, there was a national consensus that war should be avoided at almost any cost. There are also other, positive aspects to his earlier political career to consider, his success in balancing the books as Chancellor of the Exchequer in 1923-4 and his social reforms as Minister of Health, particularly during Baldwin's second premiership of 1924-29.

'Everything that I have worked for, everything that I have hoped for, everything that I have believed in during my public life, has crashed into ruins.'

Neville Chamberlain, 3 September 1939

SIR WINSTON CHURCHILL

Born:	30 November 1874
Died:	24 January 1965
Dates in Office:	10 May 1940 – 26 July 1945
	26 October 1951 – 5 April 1955
Party:	Conservative

Winston Churchill with Tommy-Gun, 1940. *CN 11/6 (24)*

Winston Churchill understood the value of a strong personal image, and how trademark features could help to project reassurance and positivity during difficult times, hence the homburg hat, the white spotted bow tie, and the cigar. Some of these features are present in this famous photograph of Churchill (wearing a tall bowler hat) with a Thompson submachine gun, which was used by the British to project him as a strong war leader, and by the Nazi regime to portray him as a gangster. And of course, we shouldn't forget to mention the victory sign, which is so closely associated with him.

Churchill exhibits the Victory Sign, 1944. *INF 1/244*

As Chris Wrigley has written, 'Churchill brought to 10 Downing Street his near-hyperactivity which, while it had some negative results was generally valuable in energising higher government'. His energy and dynamism is reflected in thousands of personal minutes and telegrams held by The National Archives, many of which are very hard-hitting and pithy, as in the Personal Minute shown below, in which he asks a series of staccato questions about the disastrous Dieppe Raid; but in some instances they also reflect Churchill's sense of playfulness.

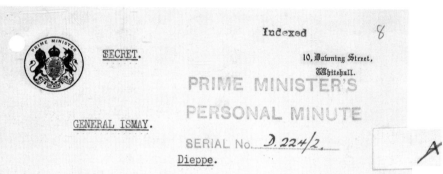

Churchill writes to General Ismay about the Dieppe Raid, 21 December 1942. *PREM 3/256*

Other documents demonstrate Churchill's force of character in rather amusing ways.

10

2

W.P. (G) (40) 211 of 9th August, 1940

To do our work, we all have to read a mass of papers. Nearly all of them are far too long. This wastes time, while energy has to be spent in looking for the essential points.

I ask my colleagues and their staffs to see to it that their Reports are shorter.

(i) The aim should be Reports which set out the main points in a series of short, crisp paragraphs.

(ii) If a Report relies on detailed analysis of some complicated factors, or on statistics, these should be set out in an Appendix.

(iii) Often the occasion is best met by submitting not a full-dress Report, but an *Aide-mémoire* consisting of headings only, which can be expanded orally if needed.

(iv) Let us have an end of such phrases as these: " It is also of importance to bear in mind the following considerations . . . .", or " Consideration should be given to the possibility of carrying into effect . . . ." Most of these woolly phrases are mere padding which can be left out altogether, or replaced by a single word. Let us not shrink from using the short expressive phrase, even if it is conversational.

Reports drawn up on the lines I propose may at first seem rough as compared with the flat surface of officialese jargon. But the saving in time will be great, while the discipline of setting out the real points concisely will prove an aid to clearer thinking.

W. S. C.

Churchill on the subject of brevity in official documents in 1940. *PREM 11/1734*

Churchill certainly made significant mistakes during his long career in government, for example his role in the disastrous Dardanelles campaign of 1915-16, specifically the landings in Gallipoli. His role in the Bengal famine of 1943 has attracted considerable controversy. However, while awareness of his flaws is more widespread in modern times, he remains widely revered, and the consensus among historians is that his role in ruling out peace mediation with Germany in 1940 was crucial; and that he was effective and resolute as a war leader, rallying the nation with his superb oratory.

In the post-war years, Churchill warned of the threat to Western interests and values posed by the Soviet Union (see an extract from his 'Iron Curtain' speech on the following page); he also gave support to the cause of European unity.

He returned to power, at the age of seventy-six, in October 1951, and continued to concentrate mainly on foreign policy, pressing the US for an international summit with the Soviet Union (which did not materialise). Churchill's health was in decline. He made a good recovery from a stroke in 1953, but in 1955 he finally retired, handing over to Anthony Eden.

Churchill remained a back bencher until 1964 – it is incredible to reflect that his Commons career had begun in 1900. Churchill died on 24 January 1965 at his London home, and he was given a state funeral.

'Now this is not the end. It is not even the beginning of the end. But it is, perhaps, the end of the beginning.' (Winston Churchill, referring to the significant Allied victory at the second battle of El Alamein, 1942)

- 5 -

From Stettin in the Baltic to Trieste in the Adriatic, an iron curtain has descended across the continent.
Behind that line lie all the capitals of the ancient states of
Central and Eastern Europe. Warsaw, Berlin, Prague, Vienna,
Budapest, Belgrade, Bucharest and Sofia, all these famous
cities and the populations around them lie in the Soviet sphere
and all are subject in one form or another, not only to Soviet
influence but to a very high and increasing measure of control
from Moscow. Athens alone, with its immortal glories, is free
to decide its future at an election under British, American and
French observation. The Russian-dominated Polish Government
has been encouraged to make enormous and wrongful inroads upon
Germany, and mass expulsions of millions of Germans on a scale
grievous and undreamed-of are now taking place. The Communist
parties, which were very small in all these Eastern States of
Europe, have been raised to pre-eminence and power far beyond
their numbers and are seeking everywhere to obtain totalitarian
control. Police governments are prevailing in nearly every
case, and so far, except in Czechoslovakia, there is no true
democracy. Turkey and Persia are both profoundly alarmed
and disturbed at the claims which are made upon them and
at the pressure being exerted by the Moscow Government. An
attempt is being made by the Russians in Berlin to build up
a quasi-Communist party in their zone of Occupied Germany
by showing special favors to groups of left-wing German
leaders. At the end of the fighting last June, the American
and British Armies withdrew Westwards, in accordance with an
earlier agreement, to a depth at some points of 150 miles
on a front of nearly 400 miles to allow the Russians to
occupy this vast expanse of territory which the Western
Democracies had conquered. If now the Soviet Government
tries, by separate action, to build up a pro-Communist Germany in their areas, this will cause new serious difficulties
in the British and American zones, and will give the defeated
Germans the power of putting themselves up to auction between
the Soviets and the Western Democracies. Whatever conclusions may be drawn from these facts - and facts they
are - this is certainly not the Liberated Europe we fought
to build up. Nor is it one which contains the essentials
of permanent peace.

(more)

Churchill's 'Iron Curtain' speech, delivered in Fulton, Missouri on 5 March 1946. *FO 371/51624*

CLEMENT ATTLEE

Born: 3 January 1883
Died: 8 October 1967
Dates in Office: 26 July 1945 – 26 October 1951
Party: Labour

Clement Attlee circa 1945. *INF 14/19*

Mention Clement Attlee to any reasonably well-informed person with an interest in modern history and they are likely to quote one or two wittily crafted insults about him, both attributed (probably incorrectly) to Churchill: 'He is a modest man, with much to be modest about' and 'An empty taxi arrived at 10 Downing Street, and when the door was opened, Mr Attlee got out'. These barbs have remained high in historical consciousness because Attlee was famously low-key and unassuming, at times almost comical with his

PRIME MINISTER

You asked for the Lord President's views on the proposal that a Bill to amend the National Health Service Act, 1946 should be introduced at the beginning of next Session.

The Lord President agrees that this is desirable and comments that the Ministry of Health will have to move quickly if it is to be possible.

This being so, you may wish to instruct Mr. Johnston to put pressure on the Ministry of Health as suggested in the last paragraph of his letter to me of the 6th September.

8th September, 1950

Attlee's response on this memo, written in blue pencil, 'Yes, CRA [Clement Richard Attlee] 8.9.50', is typically concise and indicates that he was a brisk dispenser of business. *PREM 8/1486*

conciseness. This was illustrated by his response to a BBC reporter who asked him if he wanted to make a comment about the campaign on the eve of the 1951 general election. Attlee simply replied, 'No, thank you.'

Attlee was unlikely material for a socialist leader: the product of an upper-middle class home in Putney, promoted to Major during the First World War, he loved cricket and smoked a pipe. In many respects he appeared conventional and conservative, with a small 'c'.

However, this portrayal does not give the full picture. He was, after all, leader of one of the most radical peacetime governments of the twentieth century, which transformed British society. Attlee was a formidable political operator, with passionately held convictions. From 1906 to 1909, he took on social work in the east end of London which brought him to socialism and the Labour Party.

Attlee's role in the wartime coalition government, as Lord Privy Seal, and then Deputy Prime Minister to Churchill, is often overlooked. He was incredibly efficient in his chairing of meetings, and handling of paperwork, brisk and decisive, and this highly competent approach was to become a hallmark of his premiership.

Attlee's Labour Party successfully caught the public mood in the general election of July 1945, promising 'a land fit for heroes'. The result was a stunning landslide victory. The achievements of the Labour Governments of 1945-51 were remarkable, including the creation of the National Health Service and the establishment of the modern welfare state, with the introduction of extensive sickness and unemployment cover. Major sectors of industry were taken into public ownership, including the coal and steel industries, the electricity and gas supply, the railways, and the Bank of England. Foreign Secretary Ernest Bevin was a driving force behind the creation of the North Atlantic Treaty Organisation (NATO), the military alliance for the countries of the West created as a counterweight to the Soviet Union. The Labour Government also granted India independence.

Following this period of intense activity on a grand scale, by 1951 the Labour government was exhausted, and it lost the election of October that year.

'There were few who thought him a starter, many who thought themselves smarter. But he ended PM, CH and OM, an Earl and a Knight of the Garter.'

(Self-penned limerick), Clement Attlee

ANTHONY EDEN

Born: 12 June 1897
Died: 14 January 1977
Dates in Office: 6 April 1955 – 9 January 1957
Party: Conservative

Anthony Eden. *INF 3/75 Pt 3*

In late August 1956, pressures were mounting during the Suez Crisis. In July, Egyptian leader Colonel Nasser had nationalised the Suez Canal. The bulk of Western Europe's oil was transported through the canal, as well as a good deal of trade for Commonwealth countries; Eden was determined to reverse Nasser's action and establish control of this crucial route. Eden became obsessed with the notion that Nasser was another Mussolini, who should definitely not be appeased, but faced down most strongly (and if possible, overthrown). The consensus among historians is that he misapplied the lessons of history.

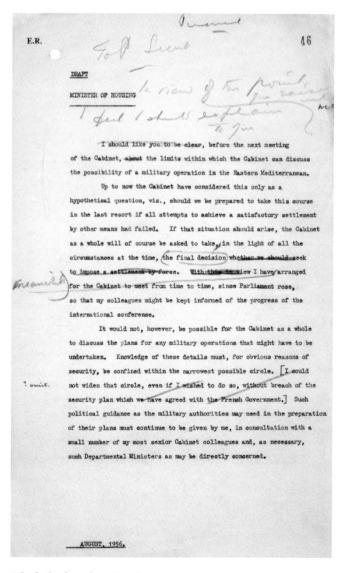

Eden's draft reply to Sandys circa 22 August 1956. *PREM 11/1152*

Diplomatic negotiations were underway but Eden secretly colluded with France (and, later, Israel) to launch an attack on Egypt. The Cabinet considered the use of force as a hypothetical question, as a last resort if all else failed, but no details had been discussed around the Cabinet table. On 23 August, Cabinet Minister Duncan Sandys wrote to Eden expressing the hope that the Cabinet as a whole would 'be consulted as soon as possible about the broad lines of the military plan which is being prepared'. He was clearly concerned that Eden might suddenly move ahead without full consultation.

Cabinet Secretary Norman Brook drafted this note for the Prime Minister, as a reply to Sandys. The two crucial sentences are: 'knowledge of these details must, for obvious reasons of security, be confined within the narrowest possible circle. [I could not widen that circle, even if I wished to, without breach of the security plan which we have agreed with the French Government]'. This second sentence (shown above in square brackets) was omitted from the final version sent to Sandys. The implication that something underhand was going on is unescapable.

In mid-October, the British, French and Israeli governments came to a confidential agreement that Israel would launch an attack on the Egyptian frontier. Britain and France would then call for both sides to withdraw from the Canal zone. Egypt was very likely to refuse to do this; British and French forces would then intervene and take control of the Canal zone.

Aerial view of the Suez operation, 1956. *ADM 195/122*

Anthony Eden, 1953. *CO 1069/893 (15)*

Israel attacked Egypt on 29 October, and Anglo-French forces landed on 5 November. A huge diplomatic row erupted. The United States reacted furiously and applied massive pressure on Britain to withdraw, and refused to support sterling which was in trouble in the exchange markets. Eden halted the operation on 6 November, the day after it had begun. It was a national humiliation for Britain and a personal disaster for Eden, who had been suffering with illness since 1953, and whose health was now in significant decline. In late November, he flew to Jamaica to recuperate but, soon after he returned, he resigned.

Anthony Eden had been Foreign Secretary three times. In the 1930s many people saw him as 'the golden boy of British politics', who, with his 'film star' looks, acquired a glamorous image. He had carefully built up his reputation for skilled diplomacy over many years. However, he destroyed this reputation though a foreign policy disaster, despite all his apparent expertise. The irony here does not need underlining. His name will always be linked with Suez.

> 'There is no doubt in our minds that Nasser, whether he likes it or not, is now effectively in Russian hands, just as Mussolini was in Hitler's. It would be as ineffective to show weakness to Nasser now in order to placate him as it was to show weakness to Mussolini.'
>
> Anthony Eden

HAROLD MACMILLAN

Born:	10 February 1894
Died:	29 December 1986
Dates in Office:	10 January 1957 – 18 October 1963
Party:	Conservative

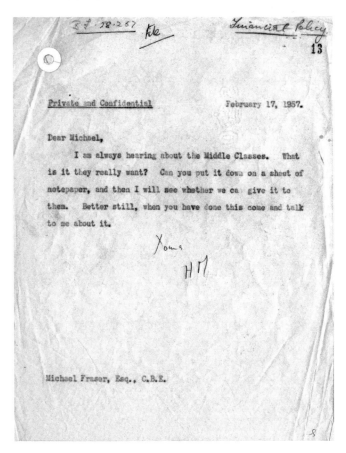

Harold Macmillan to Michael Fraser, 17 February 1957.
PREM 11/1816

Harold Macmillan's note referring to the 'middle classes' to Michael Fraser of the Conservative Research Department of 17 February 1957 is surprisingly direct: 'What is it they really want?', he asks. A prosperous middle class was an essential part of Conservative strategy. An economic boom in the late 1950s led to a rise in living standards, and although Macmillan tried to warn about the dangers of inflation, a phrase he used in a speech in July 1957 came to dominate the national discourse: 'most of our people have never had it so good'.

Macmillan's landslide general election victory in October 1959 represented an amazing transformation in the fortunes of the Conservative party, when contrasted with the tribulations surrounding the Suez crisis in late 1956 and Eden's subsequent resignation.

Macmillan's 'Winds of Change' speech delivered in South Africa in 1960 heralded an acceleration in decolonisation, and he was successful in cultivating the 'special relationship' with the United States through his warm relations with President Kennedy.

Harold Macmillan is invested as a Paramount Chief, Northern Transvaal, South Africa, February 1960. *CO 1069/1/3*

However, on the domestic front, he ran into difficulties. In the late 1950s and early 1960s, the economy overheated and the government had to apply restraining measures, due to fears about inflation. Measures such as Chancellor Selwyn Lloyd's 'Pay Pause' in 1961 (essentially a pay freeze for the public sector), and a credit squeeze were unpopular. On 15 March 1962, the Liberals seized the previously safe Conservative seat of Orpington in their first by-election victory for four years.

Macmillan took heed of this shock result and started developing new strategies for governing and handling the economy. He developed an argument on these lines: if everyone could be made to feel that they had a stake in an incomes policy, this would keep inflation under control, the cost of borrowing could be brought down, and there could be more public expenditure on housing and enhanced benefits for the needy. But his ambitious plans for this 'new approach' were overtaken by events with the dramatic mass sacking of Cabinet Ministers in July 1962, and a series of difficult events in 1963: General de Gaulle's veto of the British application for EEC membership in January; the Profumo scandal over the summer months; and Macmillan's illness in October which led him to stand down as Prime Minister.

> 'Most of our people have never had it so good.'
>
> Harold Macmillan

SIR ALEC DOUGLAS-HOME

Born: 2 July 1903
Died: 9 October 1995
Dates in Office: 19 October 1963 – 16 October 1964
Party: Conservative

In December 1963, Sir Michael Fraser, Director of the Conservative Research Department asked the Prime Minister, Sir Alec Douglas-Home, if he could let him have some notes on his general philosophy, as these could be helpful for speech writing purposes. Sir Alec duly obliged, and an extract is shown above. What comes across from reading this statement is that the outlook of this Prime Minister was straightforward and inspired by a strong sense of duty and fundamental decency, reflecting clear-sighted thinking. And by common consensus, these were qualities that Douglas-Home, the 14th Earl of Home (who renounced his hereditary title in 1963 so he could sit in the House of Commons) had in strong measure. This is an assessment at variance with the out-of-touch, grouse moor loving, aristocratic caricature which the Leader of the Opposition Harold Wilson was able to pin on him.

The only Prime Minister to have held office for less time than Douglas-Home was Andrew Bonar Law. Does this make him another candidate for the unfortunate epithet 'the least remembered Prime Minister of the twentieth century'? He is certainly in the running for this. However, although he had limited time to make an impression, he had his share of achievements. Sir Alec successfully backed the abolition of resale price maintenance (fixed prices for products) – a significant domestic reform which led to cheaper prices for goods through increased competition.

However, his greatest strength was foreign policy (he had served as Commonwealth Secretary and Foreign Secretary before becoming Prime Minister). When conflict broke out in Cyprus between the Greek and Turkish Cypriots in August 1964, Douglas-Home brought effective diplomatic pressure to help bring about a ceasefire.

Sir Alec was an uncomfortable performer on television and this factor, combined with his privileged background, made him an easy target for lampooning, especially during the

Bf 14/1/64

Mr Wright to see

Subject file

5

10, Downing Street,
Whitehall,

Prime Minister's
Personal Minute
No. M.48 H/63.

SIR MICHAEL FRASER

I went into politics because I felt that it was a form
of public service and that as nearly a generation of
politicians had been cut down in the first war those who had
anything to give in the way of leadership ought to do so.

I was convinced that the Conservative philosophy of life
was right and the Socialist recipes for equality were merely
another way of saying that the pace of the slowest would
govern our affairs so I went in to lend a hand.

I have always thought it to be touch and go whether
democracy (one man one vote) will last. Certainly it will
relapse into some more authoritarian form of government unless
the great majority are really well educated in the basic facts
of community and international living. At present the
British people decide by instinct rather than reason and while
that period lasts leadership is all important. The
Conservatives can give it - the Socialists cannot.

People who live close to nature act by instinct
reinforced by deduction. They are natural conservatives -
slow thinkers but sound. They get pretty close to true
values. It is the townspeople with few roots as yet who need
constant leadership. It is, however, they, who have the votes
who will sway the election decision.

I took on the job of Prime Minister because throughout my
political career I have done what I have been asked to do when
I thought it my duty. But a large part in my decision was
the feeling that only by simple straightforward talk to the
industrial masses could we hope to defeat the Socialists.

"My philosophy": Sir Alec Douglas-Home to Sir Michael Fraser. *PREM 11/5006*

Sir Alec Douglas-Home, March 1964. *INF 10/253*

satire boom of the early 1960s. Nonetheless, his integrity still shone through, and he came close to winning the October 1964 general election. And politics was not his only interest by any means: historian Andrew Holt has pointed out that he remains the only Prime Minister to have played first-class cricket. Charm was another of his qualities: Sir Alec concluded his 'my philosophy' statement with these words: 'Is this enough for a first instalment, and is there enough of "me" in it? Anyway, I am bored with myself for the time being!' – a nice, self-deprecating touch.

> 'There are two problems in my life. The political ones are insoluble and the economic ones are incomprehensible.'
>
> Sir Alec Douglas-Home

HAROLD WILSON

Born: 11 March 1916
Died: 24 May 1995
Dates in Office: 16 October 1964 – 19 June 1970,
                 4 March 1974 – 5 April 1976
Party: Labour

Harold Wilson at National Coal Board Gala, 1950. *COAL 80/1119*

If I had to single out just one appealing quality associated with Harold Wilson I would choose his wit. He could use this to great political effect, with dazzling style. A great example of this is an audacious joke he made during a speech on 4 May 1969. His premiership had been going through a very troubled period and there were rumours of ministerial plots to dislodge him from office. 'I know what is going on,' he declared – then he paused. His audience was rapt with attention. Then he said, '*I* am going on' and there was a barrage of laughter from the floor.

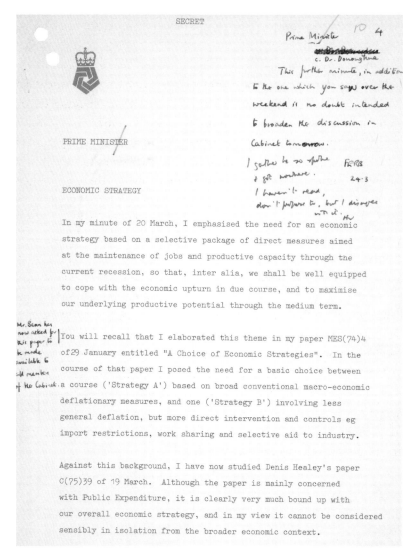

Harold Wilson's comment ('I haven't read...') can be seen on Tony Benn's memo, March 1975. *PREM 16/341*

This sophisticated wit shows itself in the public records, albeit intended for a limited audience at the time of its creation. During the mid-1970s, Cabinet Minister Tony Benn urged Wilson to adopt an alternative economic strategy. When Wilson received a memo from Benn on these lines in March 1975, the Prime Minister's comment was a model of conciseness: 'I haven't read, don't propose to, but I disagree with it'.

Harold Wilson is notable for several other reasons. He led the Labour Party to victory in four general elections (1964, 1966, followed by a comeback in 1974 when he won two elections). After becoming Labour leader in early 1963 following the untimely death of Hugh Gaitskell, Wilson was successful in projecting an image with classless appeal, with a strong impression of dynamism. He promised a vision of a new Britain, 'forged in the white heat' of a scientific, economic and social revolution. It can be argued that his governments of 1964-70 failed to deliver on these heady promises; instead, the government wrestled with a series of sterling crises, had to abandon its grand plans for the economy, introduced deep cuts and suffered a humiliating devaluation of the pound in 1967.

However, there was also a positive record of achievements. His governments introduced liberal social policies, including the abolition of capital punishment, the (partial) decriminalisation of homosexuality and reform of abortion law. There was a huge expansion of higher education, and the Open University was established. It has been said by some that Wilson's greatest achievement was keeping British troops out of Vietnam.

Wilson is often portrayed as tired and disengaged during his 'swansong' period as Prime Minister in 1974-76, struggling to respond effectively to the problem of mounting inflation. Again, though, an important argument in Wilson's favour can be made. In 1975, he successfully called a referendum about whether Britain should stay in the European Economic Community on the basis of renegotiated terms, or leave. The Labour Party was badly split on this issue, but Wilson handled the campaign with great skill, suspending Cabinet collective responsibility so that ministers could campaign for staying or for leaving the EEC, as their consciences dictated. He thus held the Labour Party together and his approach was vindicated by a sizable 'yes' vote for remaining, his desired outcome.

Wilson caused a political shockwave on 16 March 1976 when he announced he was to resign, five days after his 60th birthday. Very few people had known, but he had actually been planning to do this from as early as March 1974.

'A week is a long time in politics.'

Harold Wilson

EDWARD HEATH

Born:	9 July 1916
Died :	17 July 2005
Dates in Office:	19 June 1970 – 4 March 1974
Party:	Conservative

While Edward ('Ted') Heath was passionate about classical music (and an accomplished musician), his attendance at a pop concert seems an incongruous notion. However, here we see a letter of thanks from Heath to Lord Harlech, organiser of a Steeleye Span concert which he had attended at the Royal Albert Hall. An official, obviously concerned at the prospect, had suggested beforehand that the Prime Minister need stay only for a very short time and that the Prime Minister 'should be at some distance from active audience participation'. The concert was part of the 'Fanfare for Europe' programme of celebrations in January 1973 which marked the entry of the United Kingdom into the European Economic Community.

Taking the United Kingdom into Europe was a great personal triumph for Heath. As Dick Leonard has written, 'it is doubtful whether any other Prime Minister, in the circumstances of the time … could have pulled it off'. Heath's cultivation of the French President Georges Pompidou was crucial to the process. Not everyone would agree about this being his government's greatest achievement, but it was certainly its most important legacy.

By contrast, the shorthand version of Heath as Prime Minister was that he presided over dramatic U-turns in economic and industrial policy, worrying levels of inflation, miners' strikes, power cuts and the three-day week before falling from power.

Heath sought logical and rational solutions to the nation's problems but this approach could amount to inflexibility; and he was not a natural communicator, appearing 'wooden' on television. However, he was not necessarily the author of all of his misfortune.

It can be argued that Heath was unlucky. Looking back to the spring of 1973, the government's 'Programme for Controlling Inflation', which involved statutory controls on

6c9

10 Downing Street
Whitehall

18 January 1973

Dear David,

Thank you very much for inviting me to the
Steeleye Span Band concert at the Albert Hall.   I
was very glad to see the other half of the Fanfare
for Europe celebration and much enjoyed the
performance.

I am most grateful to you for the amount of
work you put in on the pop side of Fanfare for Europe,
the success of which has added greatly to the Fanfare
celebrations.

Yours ever,

Ted

The Rt. Hon. The Lord Harlech, K.C.M.G.

M

Edward Heath to Lord Harlech, 18 January 1973. *PREM 15/1489*

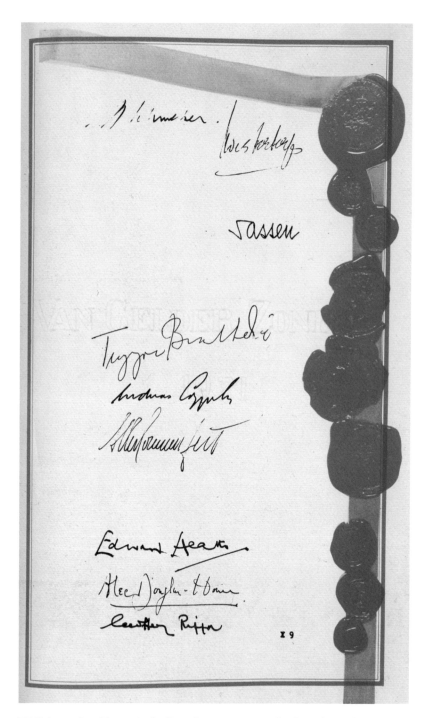

EEC Accession Treaty including the signatures of Edward Heath, Sir Alec Douglas-Home, and Geoffrey Rippon, 22 January 1972. *FO 949/146*

Right: **Edward Heath, 1966.** *National Archives and Records Administration, USA*

Below: **The Amir of Bahrain meets Edward Heath, 1973.** *INF 14/423*

pay and prices, seemed to be having the desired effect of curbing price rises. However, Heath could not have predicted the Yom Kippur War (also known as the fourth Arab-Israeli War) which broke out in October 1973.

This conflict was followed by restrictions on oil supplies and the quadrupling of oil prices – as a result, there was a premium attached to coal, and the miners, wanting to take advantage of this, then put in a sizable pay claim which the government refused. The end result of this impasse was a strike, as Heath refused to make the miners a special case. He staked his reputation on a defence of his statutory incomes policy but lost the general election of February 1974, and failed to win the following election of October that year. He lost the Conservative Party leadership contest in February 1975 and was succeeded by Margaret Thatcher, but he found this turn of events difficult to come to terms with, and began what became known as 'the longest sulk in history'.

'We shall have a harder Christmas than we have known since the war.'

Edward Heath, December 1973.

JAMES CALLAGHAN

Born: 27 March 1912
Died: 26 March 2005
Dates in office: 5 April 1976 – 4 May 1979
Party: Labour

James Callaghan's notes, September 1978. *PREM 16/1667*

James ('Jim') Callaghan wrote some 27 pages of notes for a meeting on future policy initiatives on 19 September 1978, and this extract is illuminating about his short premiership and his surprise (and highly significant) decision to defer the general election which he had announced on 7 September. It is certainly defensive in tone, but also reflects a stubborn pride about how he has repeatedly confounded the 'doomsayers' over the years. Let's deconstruct it line by line.

It begins, 'I've been written off more times than I care to remember' and continues:'1. In March 76 - they said an election in the autumn'. He is referring to becoming Prime Minister following the Harold Wilson's unexpected public announcement on 16 March 1976 that he was resigning as Prime Minister. Callaghan inherited a government with a very small majority which he lost on his first full day in office, hence the predictions of a short-lived premiership from 'they' (he has the Conservative Party and the press in mind).

Next, he writes: '2. At Oct 76 Conference I had delivered my 1st and last speech as PM'. Callaghan's speech at the Labour conference in Blackpool had actually delivered on 28 September 1976. At that time, his government was under massive pressure – it had been forced to apply for a loan from the International Monetary Fund for 3.9 billion dollars, there was a sterling crisis, and the prospect of ever deeper cuts in public expenditure.

For point no.3, the Prime Minister writes: 'In March '77 [prior to the arrangement with Libs] we would be forced to go to the country then'. On March 23 1977, the Labour and Liberal parties agreed the 'Lib-Lab' pact, which enabled the Labour government to stay in power. Whilst Callaghan recalls the naysayers predicting an election in October that year (point no.4), the pact brought a period of stability which saw a significant improvement in the economy, and the agreement lasted until August 1978. A key part of the government's strategy was a voluntary pay policy to limit pay increases as a means of reducing inflation.

With point no.5, Callaghan brought the situation up to date: 'then they decided they would fix the Election for October '78'. A general election that autumn had been widely expected, not just by the Conservative Party and the press, but by Labour Party members and the public. The economic indicators looked promising – inflation had peaked at 26 per cent during Wilson's premiership in 1975 and by 1978 it had fallen to 8 per cent. However, the Prime Minister, ruminating over polling data at his Sussex farm in August, decided to defer and soldier on through the winter, determined to stick to a pay increases limit of 5 per cent. He kept his cards close to his chest, famously teasing the Trade Union Congress by singing the music hall ditty 'Waiting at the Church'. When Callaghan announced his decision to the public on 7 September, many were astounded. 'Neither the press nor the Tory Party will fix it', he concludes – the calling of the election is his prerogative, his alone, is his defiant statement – though eventually an election was forced upon him.

Callaghan's decision not to call an election in the autumn of 1978 is often referred to as his greatest mistake, as what lay in store was the 'Winter of Discontent' of December 1978 to

James Callaghan, Shadow Home Secretary, and James Chichester-Clark, Prime Minister of Northern Ireland, August 1970. *National Archives of the Netherlands*

mid-March 1979, a wave of seriously disruptive strikes across the public sector, as unions refused to comply with the 5 per cent pay norm. This calamity coincided with a bitterly cold winter. Callaghan and his government were thoroughly demoralised and press coverage was ferocious. On 28 March 1979, the government was defeated by 311 votes to 310 on an opposition motion of no confidence. Labour lost the general election which followed and Margaret Thatcher came to power; the Conservatives were to stay in power for 18 years.

The document example analysed above is a revealing piece of marginalia, but it would be wrong to give the impression that James Callaghan proceeded through life in an embittered and defensive manner. After all, he acquired the nickname 'Sunny Jim', for his amiability. For the greater part of his premiership, he successfully projected a strong image of unflappability and competence, and this was reflected in his personal opinion poll ratings, which remained strong. He was thoroughly grounded in the art of government, being the only Prime Minister to have previously held the three major offices of state, Chancellor of the Exchequer, Home Secretary and Foreign Secretary. Callaghan was clearly patriotic, and he had served in the Royal Navy during the Second World War.

For a long time he frequently triumphed over opposition leader Thatcher in the House of Commons, using wit as an effective weapon, though by February 1979, with scenes of widespread industrial chaos, he was forced onto the defensive – the die was cast – a 'sea change' was on its way, and it was for Mrs Thatcher, as Callaghan predicted towards the end of the election campaign.

> 'When I am shaving in the morning, I say to myself that if I were a young man I would emigrate.'
>
> James Callaghan (Cabinet strategy meeting at Chequers, 17 November 1974).

MARGARET THATCHER

Born: 13 October 1925
Died: 8 April 2013
Dates in Office: 4 May 1979 – 28 November 1990
Party: Conservative

Margaret Thatcher. *PREM 19/1310*

There is a scene in the film *The Iron Lady* (2011) when Margaret Thatcher (played by Meryl Streep) is shown gazing intensely at a typed memo, underlining particular sections with a blue felt tip pen. This aspect was pleasing to see as it is wholly accurate, as evidenced in the Prime Minister's Office records. Thatcher's underlining was evidence of a laser-like focus on the details of the matter in hand.

As Prime Minister, Mrs Thatcher was passionate about her mission to bring about change on several fronts. This determination reveals itself in forthright handwritten comments. Sometimes her anger was directed at other parts of government, as she voiced her frustration at encountering obstacles.

A classic example of marginalia (see next page) illustrates this point. From late 1979 onwards, Mrs Thatcher took a tough stance in negotiating a reduction in Britain's net contribution to the European Economic Community (EEC) budget. When the Foreign and Commonwealth Office produced a draft statement on North Sea oil which hinted at making some concessions to the EEC, she wrote: 'that statement would be disastrous for Britain and I am not prepared to make it. The idea that we should have to sacrifice our main assets to secure some of our own money back is one that may appeal to the Foreign Office but it doesn't to me. Wouldn't it have been courteous to say the least to have come to me first?' Her fury is palpable.

It can be argued that, if Mrs Thatcher had not been so fiercely combative at key moments, she might not have achieved as much as she did, in terms of bringing about change. However, her legacy is contested. Margaret Thatcher remains the most divisive figure in Britain's modern political history. She was also the United Kingdom's first female Prime Minister and the longest serving British holder of that office during the twentieth century.

Mrs Thatcher came to power in May 1979, a conviction politician determined to dismantle the post-1945 consensus, though her radical zeal was tempered with caution in some respects. Her government established a new course for the economy, summed up by the umbrella term 'monetarism'. In essence, this meant tight control of the money supply in order to conquer inflation, which necessitated cuts in public spending and high interest rates.

The first three years in power were very difficult, as unemployment soared and, in the summer of 1981, riots broke out in several cities. Mrs Thatcher became an unpopular figure for many. However, victory in the Falklands War transformed the political landscape and Thatcher went on to win election victories in 1983 and 1987.

Thatcher rolled back the frontiers of the state, as her governments pursued the radical policy of privatising government-owned industries, and swathes of regulation were swept away, as the economy was reshaped in accordance with her free market approach. Trade Union reform was also an important element of her strategy. The failure of the miners' strike (1984-85) was a watershed in industrial relations.

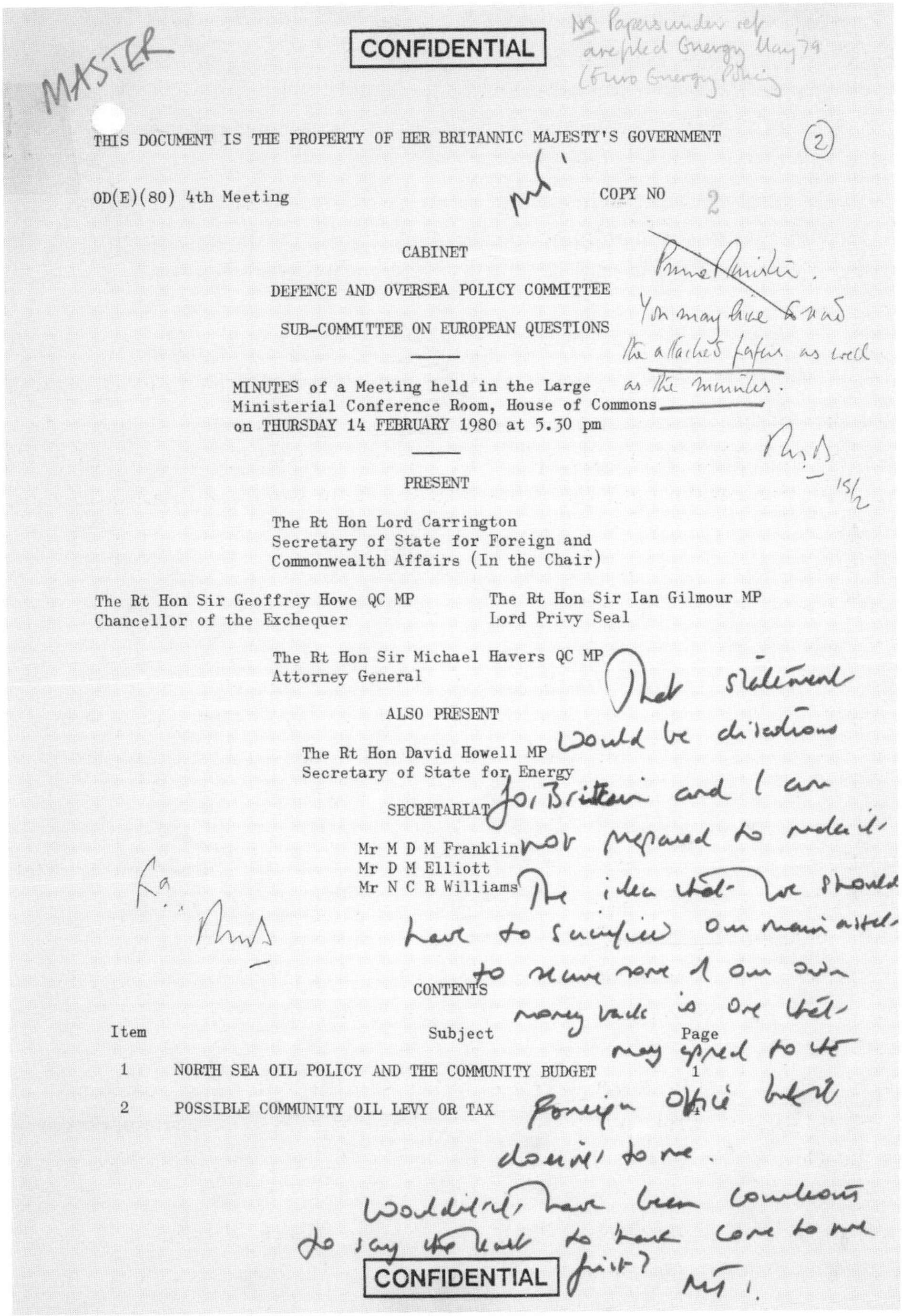

CONFIDENTIAL

THIS DOCUMENT IS THE PROPERTY OF HER BRITANNIC MAJESTY'S GOVERNMENT

②

OD(E)(80) 4th Meeting

COPY NO 2

CABINET

DEFENCE AND OVERSEA POLICY COMMITTEE

SUB-COMMITTEE ON EUROPEAN QUESTIONS

———

MINUTES of a Meeting held in the Large
Ministerial Conference Room, House of Commons
on THURSDAY 14 FEBRUARY 1980 at 5.30 pm

———

PRESENT

The Rt Hon Lord Carrington
Secretary of State for Foreign and
Commonwealth Affairs (In the Chair)

The Rt Hon Sir Geoffrey Howe QC MP   The Rt Hon Sir Ian Gilmour MP
Chancellor of the Exchequer   Lord Privy Seal

The Rt Hon Sir Michael Havers QC MP
Attorney General

ALSO PRESENT

The Rt Hon David Howell MP
Secretary of State for Energy

SECRETARIAT

Mr M D M Franklin
Mr D M Elliott
Mr N C R Williams

CONTENTS

Item	Subject	Page
1	NORTH SEA OIL POLICY AND THE COMMUNITY BUDGET	1
2	POSSIBLE COMMUNITY OIL LEVY OR TAX	4

CONFIDENTIAL

Handwritten annotations:

MS Papers under ref are filed Energy May '79 (Two Energy Policy)

Prime Minister.
You may have to read the attached paper as well as the minutes.
RW ― 15/2

That statement would be disastrous for Britain and I am not prepared to make it. The idea that we should have to sacrifice our main article to secure some of our own money back is one that may appeal to the Foreign Office but it doesn't to me. Wouldn't it have been courteous to say the least to have come to me first? MT.

Margaret Thatcher responds to a Foreign Office statement regarding North Sea Oil, **14 February 1980.** *PREM 19/223*

Margaret Thatcher forged a close alliance with US President Ronald Reagan. As a Cold War warrior, Mrs Thatcher regarded her labelling by the Soviet Union as the 'Iron Lady' as a badge of honour, though she established warm relations with Mikhail Gorbachev.

Tensions over Europe, and the unpopularity of the poll tax, contributed to her sudden downfall in November 1990.

'To those waiting with bated breath for that favourite media catchphrase, the "U-turn", I have only one thing to say: "You turn if you want to. The lady's not for turning!"

Margaret Thatcher (Speech to the Conservative Party Conference on 10 October 1980).

JOHN MAJOR

Born: 29 March 1943
Dates in Office: 28 November 1990 – 2 May 1997
Party: Conservative

Sarah Hogg, Head of the No.10 Policy unit, writes to John Major on 6 August 1992 about the forthcoming Public Expenditure Survey (PES), an annual cycle in which the Treasury negotiates with each spending Minister in order to agree a set of programmes that can be fitted into the available funds. She states that the Chancellor (Norman Lamont) 'seems to be leaning towards having no committee meetings with individual colleagues', relying on the Chief Secretary to the Treasury to represent their views instead. Mrs Hogg warns against this, fearing that colleagues 'would complain of being bounced or ignored'.

In a characteristic handwritten response, Major replies: 'Yes I agree. They [would] be difficult anyway. We want "jaw, jaw", not war, war. Colleagues must have the opportunity to argue their case. Time consuming, I know – but an essential p/o [part of] the equation'. John Major's marginalia reflects his collegiate and consensual approach to the role of Prime Minister, and his emollient style was a great asset when he became Prime Minister in late November 1990. Many found this facet of his personality a refreshing contrast with the forthright tone struck by his predecessor Margaret Thatcher. It is interesting to note that Major is referencing Churchill here, who is reported as saying in 1954 that 'meeting jaw to jaw is better than war', a phrase later used by Macmillan who amended it (or misquoted it) as 'jaw, jaw is better than war, war'.

During his initial period as Prime Minister, Major enjoyed a sustained 'honeymoon'. He announced the abolition of the unpopular poll tax. In close liaison with US President George H.W. Bush, Major's handling of the first Gulf War was widely considered to be exemplary.

Despite an economic recession which took hold in 1991, Major won the general election of April 1992, a result which took some commentators by surprise. However, within a few months, Britain was forced out of the Exchange Rate Mechanism, on 'Black Wednesday'. This was a highly costly reversal of policy; however, the economy later revived strongly.

SECRET AND PERSONAL

PRIME MINISTER   6th August 1992

PUBLIC SPENDING

I touched base with the Treasury on the strategy for the PES
round. As you know, Michael Portillo's rather over-ambitious
letters have gone round. The Chancellor will want to discuss with
you what happens next. His plan, I gather privately, is as
follows. First, to have a meeting of his committee just before
he goes to Washington, which will require the Chief Secretary to
have completed his bilaterals in the first two weeks of
September.

This meeting will discuss the Chief Secretary's first stab at an
allocation. The Chancellor then seems to be leaning towards
having no committee meetings with individual colleagues, but only
with the Chief Secretary "representing their views" before
bringing the package to Cabinet. I hope he is being persuaded out
of this - I think it is not what Cabinet would have understood
was happening from the initial Cabinet discussion, and colleagues
would complain of being bounced or ignored. It would be an
impossibly difficult Cabinet for you to handle.

A better scenario, which he may be persuaded into, is to write
round to colleagues intimating the outcome of his committee's
initial discussions and inviting their views. Then (probably all)
colleagues would be given their individual chances to discuss
their allocation with his committee. The write-round could occur

Sarah Hogg writes to John Major about the forthcoming Public Expenditure Survey, 6 August 1992. *PREM 19/3686/1*

John Major, 1992. *CO 1069/899*

Although Major was proud of his negotiating record regarding the Treaty on European Union (the Maastricht Treaty), his government suffered from bitter divisions over Europe. His 'back to basics' campaign praised traditional values but was interpreted by media commentators as a stricture about morality – it then misfired due to a series of scandals, which Major addressed by setting up the Committee on Standards in Public Life.

Major's Citizen's Charter programme made public services more responsive to their users, an initiative that he cared about deeply. A highly important part of his legacy as Prime Minister was his skilful handling of Anglo-Irish relations, which paved the way for the later peace agreement.

On the morning of his defeat in the May 1997 general election, Major resigned the leadership of his party and went to watch cricket at the Oval.

'I want to see us build a country that is at ease with itself, a country that is confident and a country that is able and willing to build a better quality of life for all its citizens.'

John Major

TONY BLAIR

Born:	6 May 1953
Dates in Office:	2 May 1997 – 27 June 2007
Party:	Labour

Here we see the last page of the Northern Ireland Peace Agreement, known as the Good Friday Agreement, dated 10 April 1998 and bearing the signatures of Tony Blair and Marjorie 'Mo' Mowlam, Northern Ireland Secretary, for the Government of the United Kingdom of Great Britain and Northern Ireland, and Bertie Ahern, Taoiseach, and David Andrews, Minister for Foreign Affairs, for the Government of Ireland.

Just three days before the signing, Blair had joined the negotiations which had reached deadlock. His participation proved decisive, as his persuasive powers were a significant contributing factor to the ultimate success of the talks. Blair was willing to work long into the nights until the deal was concluded. The Agreement effectively brought an end to the Troubles, a conflict which had afflicted Northern Ireland since the late 1960s. Some elements of Blair's legacy as Prime Minister are contested, but, even though the settlement encapsulated in the Peace Agreement has been under strain at times, it remains a towering achievement.

Tony Blair is the longest serving Labour Prime Minister, winning three general elections. From 1994 onwards, his New Labour movement shifted Labour policy to the centre and, when the general election came in May 1997, Blair was able to capitalise on the prevailing desire for change in the country after eighteen years of Conservative governments, winning a huge majority. Blair's youthful image, superb communication skills and charismatic aura were all factors which contributed to his broad-based appeal. When he entered No 10, it was his first job in government, he had no ministerial experience.

Blair and his Chancellor, Gordon Brown, were the key driving forces within the government, but tensions were soon to develop between them. Brown made a bold move within days of taking office by making the Bank of England independent, though he was cautious with spending plans in the first two years. The promised extra investment in education and the NHS was to follow later. The economy enjoyed a sustained boom during the Blair years.

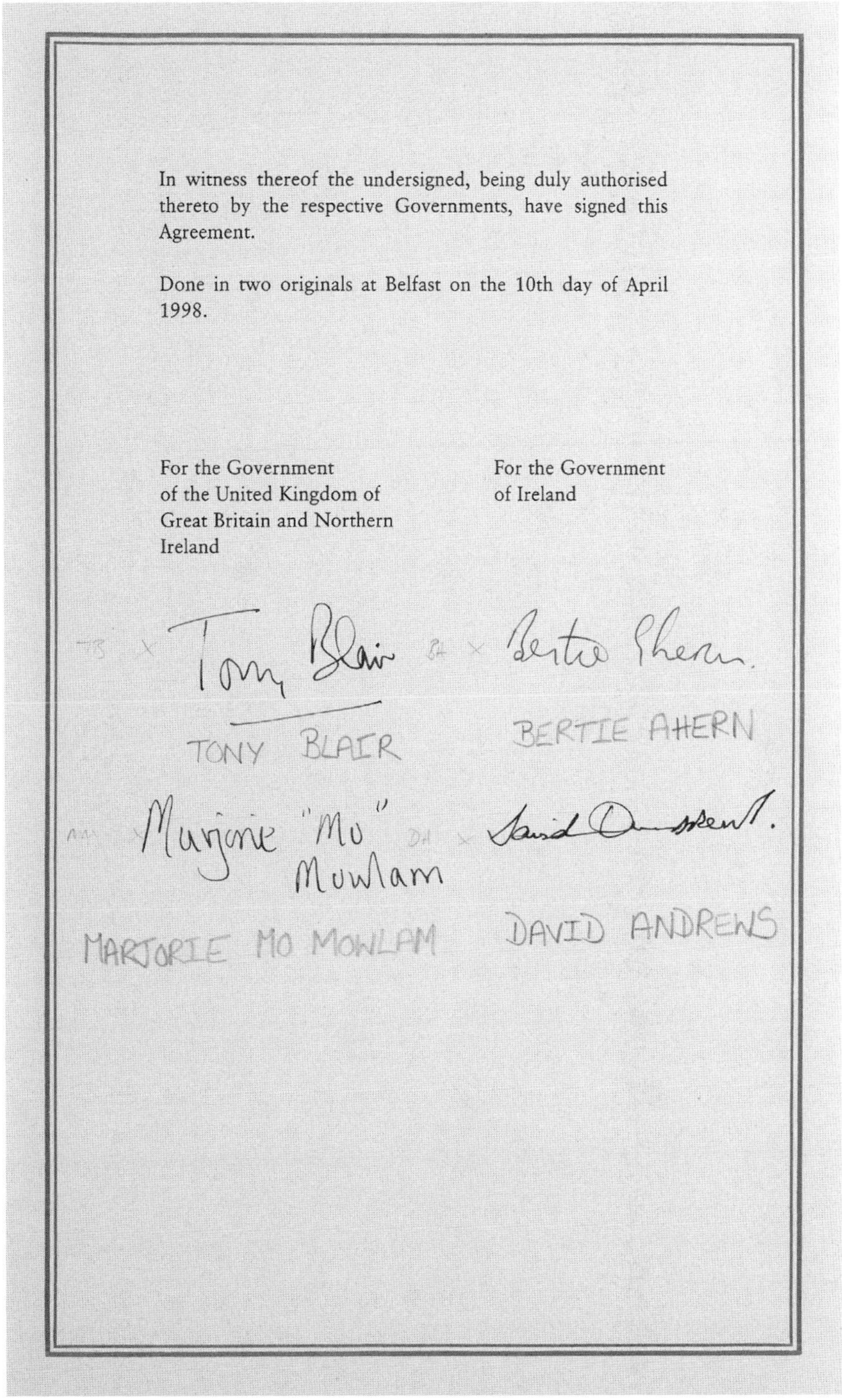

In witness thereof the undersigned, being duly authorised thereto by the respective Governments, have signed this Agreement.

Done in two originals at Belfast on the 10th day of April 1998.

For the Government of the United Kingdom of Great Britain and Northern Ireland

For the Government of Ireland

Tony Blair
TONY BLAIR
BERTIE AHERN
Marjorie "Mo" Mowlam
MARJORIE MO MOWLAM
DAVID ANDREWS

The Good Friday Agreement (Belfast Agreement), 10 April 1998. *FO 93/171/33*

Tony Blair, 2012. *Creative Commons*

The New Labour governments took a sharply focused and professional approach to media relations under Alistair Campbell, Press Secretary (later Director of Communications). This emphasis led to accusations from detractors that the government was obsessed with 'spin' rather than substance. However, tangible reforms were made on the domestic front; the minimum wage was successfully introduced, there were several legislative measures enhancing LGBT rights, and the Scottish Parliament, Welsh Assembly and the Greater London Authority including an elected Mayor were all established.

Blair backed successful humanitarian interventions in Kosovo in 1999 and Sierra Leone in 2000, and these had the effect of boosting his confidence on the world stage. After the terrorist attacks in the US on 11 September 2001, Blair was perceived as drawing close to US President George Bush. His advocacy for the invasion of Iraq, which was carried out by US and British forces in 2003, remains a controversial aspect of his premiership.

'A day like today is not a day for soundbites, we can leave those at home, but I feel the hand of history upon our shoulder with respect to this, I really do.'

(Tony Blair's statement to the press on arrival in Northern Ireland, 7 April 1998, for the negotiations which produced the Good Friday Agreement).

NOTES